VICTORIA & ALBERT

✳ ✳ ✳

THE COLOURFUL PERSONAL LIFE OF QUEEN VICTORIA – PART 2

ILLUSTRATED WITH PORTRAITS FROM THE AUTHOR'S COLLECTION

SUSAN SYMONS

FASCINATING ROYAL HISTORY

Published by Roseland Books
The Old Rectory, St Just-in-Roseland, Truro, Cornwall, TR2 5JD

Copyright ©2016 Susan Symons

ISBN 13: 978-0-9928014-5-8
ISBN 10: 0992810451

For my talented son Alexis, with happy memories of that first visit to Coburg together – many years ago.

CONTENTS

1

INTRODUCTION

Queen Victoria and Prince Albert were married at the Chapel Royal, St James's Palace in London, on 10 February 1840, when they were both twenty years old. A print of the painting of their wedding ceremony by Sir George Hayter is shown on the next page. Victoria wore a white satin wedding dress, decorated with Honiton lace, and had orange blossom in her hair. Her jewellery was a diamond necklace and earrings, and the magnificent sapphire and diamond brooch Albert had just given her as a wedding present.

Victoria had twelve bridesmaids (some of them are behind her in the illustration), and she was given away by her uncle, the duke of Sussex (the tall figure on her right wearing a cap). He cried during the ceremony. In the picture Victoria gazes adoringly at Albert. He wore the uniform of a field marshal and the Order of the Garter. For her, their marriage was the result of a whirlwind romance; for him it was the successful outcome of a long-laid plan. The marriage would succeed, but there were some stormy waters ahead.

This is the second of my three books about *The Colourful Personal Life of Queen Victoria*. For me, her story splits quite naturally into three parts. The first book, called *Young Victoria*, is the story of the early years of her life, including her difficult childhood and how she came to the throne aged eighteen. This book, called *Victoria & Albert*, looks at the middle part of her life and her marriage to Prince Albert. The third will be called *The Widowed Queen*, and cover the long years of her widowhood, after Albert's early death.

This part of Victoria's story shows how her marriage to Albert was the result of years of plotting by his family and was very unpopular with the British public. It looks at early troubles for the couple, with power struggles, personality clashes, and unwelcome pregnancies; and also how they came through these to create a true partnership and a happy family life. And it ends with the story of Albert's death, and how a man in the prime of his life was worn out by the stresses and strains of being Victoria's husband.

1. Victoria and Albert at their wedding ceremony on 10 February 1840.

My books are a personal view of Queen Victoria's life story, from many years of researching and reading about her. They are not a comprehensive account of her reign but instead focus on her as a woman – her personal life, the events that formed her character, and the relationships that were important to her. Victoria and Albert were in an unusual position in their time, because it was Victoria who was the sovereign and Albert had a supporting role. As a married queen, Victoria faced a dichotomy between her public role as head of state and her private role as Victorian wife and mother, where Albert was the head of the family. Victoria spent a third of her married life pregnant, and this book also looks at how she dealt with pregnancy, childbirth, and being a mother.

2. Victoria in her bridal robes, wearing the brooch Albert gave her as a wedding present.

The Saxe-Coburg dynasty of Great Britain

Albert was a prince of Saxe-Coburg-Gotha (shortened for ease to Saxe-Coburg in this book) and when he married Queen Victoria in 1840 this became the surname of the British royal family. Victoria and Albert founded the Saxe-Coburg dynasty of Great Britain and Queen Elizabeth II is their great-great-granddaughter.

The surname of the British royal family remained Saxe-Coburg until 1917 when, during World War I, George V changed it to the much more English-sounding Windsor (taken from Windsor castle near London) for fear of being thought too German.

As in my first book, I have used some of Victoria's own words to help tell the story of *Victoria & Albert*. The queen was a prodigious diarist and kept a daily journal from age thirteen until just a few days before she died. After Victoria's death most of the journal was destroyed by her daughter Beatrice but, as instructed by her mother, Beatrice first made an edited transcript. This does survive and is now accessible online; in total it runs to one hundred and twenty-four volumes! Victoria was also a prolific letter writer and some of her letters have been published. Most notable is the fascinating correspondence with her eldest daughter Vicky (who became empress of Germany) in which, over more than forty years, they discuss state affairs, family news, and gossip.

3. Albert at twenty years old.

My interest in Queen Victoria began many years ago after I found a portrait of her in our attic. That picture was the beginning of my collection of portraits of the queen and her family and some of these are shown as illustrations in this book. In her own times Victoria's image was portrayed everywhere, in all sorts of media – from grand state portraits by famous royal portrait painters such as Landseer, Winterhalter, and Von Angeli, to mass-produced prints and photographs for the middle classes, and satirical cartoons. One of the things I find so fascinating is how her public image changed dramatically during her reign – from the fresh and innocent young queen of *Young Victoria*, who represented a break with the past and the beginning of a new era; to the respectable matron and mother of a happy family in *Victoria and Albert*, so different an image to the scandal-ridden Hanoverians before her; to the solid, complacent, and rather tired image of *The Widowed Queen* towards the end of her reign, a symbol for Britain and the British Empire.

I want to thank the ladies of the Women's Institute (WI) in Cornwall, who have encouraged me to write *The Colourful Personal Life of Queen Victoria*. These books are based on talks I gave to branches of the WI in Cornwall, where I live. The ladies of the WI have constantly surprised me with their own memorabilia and memories of her – a pair of Victoria's knickers; a Victoria Cross given by the queen in person to one member's ancestor for valour in the Crimean War; connections with a house in Ealing in London, once owned by Victoria's father; and a first-hand account of the relationship between Victoria and her servant John Brown, told in the 1940s to the mother of a WI member by an old lady who, in her youth, was a maid at Balmoral Castle in Scotland (one of Victoria's homes).

4. *Cartes-de-visite* photo of Victoria and Albert around 1860.

Queen Victoria and photography

Victoria's reign coincided with the invention and development of photography. The first-ever photographic picture, using the process invented by the Frenchman L J M Daguerre, was taken in the same year that Victoria came to the throne (1837), and the queen saw a photograph for the first time (then called a **Daguerreotype**) on the morning of the day (in October 1839) she proposed to Albert.

The first photographs of Victoria herself were taken in 1844 or 1845 (the exact date is not known). Like other royal sitters she was used to being flattered by portrait painters (if they did not flatter they might not get another commission) so that she did not always like what she saw in her photograph. Lengthy exposure times were required at this early stage of photography (perhaps half a minute) with the result that portrait photos could often look stilted and unnatural. In the Royal Archives there is an 1852 photograph of Victoria with her five eldest children where the queen's face has been scratched out, presumably by Victoria herself because she did not like the way she looked.

Victoria and Albert gave a boost to the emerging photographic industry when they permitted photographs of the royal family to be taken in 1860 for sale as **cartes-de-visite**. These were small mounted photos, the size of a visiting card, which could be pasted into a photograph album. The resulting photos sold to the public in hundreds of thousands and started a craze for collecting and exchanging photographs.

Many of the major developments in photography were made during Victoria's reign. In 1888 the era of amateur photography began when the first, easy-to-use, **Kodak Box camera** went on sale. Some members of the royal family became keen photographers, most notably Victoria's daughter-in-law, Alexandra, princess of Wales (later Queen Alexandra). And before she died, Victoria took part in another 'first' when, in 1896, she was recorded on moving film with the tsar of Russia and his family, by the newly invented Grand Cinematograph (or **Cine camera**).

2

THE COBURG CONSPIRACY

The marriage with Albert was by no means a grand match for Victoria. As the reigning queen of a major European power, she could have had her pick of sons from the royal families of Europe. Instead she chose Albert, a prince from a minor German duchy. But for Albert and his family, it was the triumphant realisation of a plan made soon after he was born, and a major step in their dramatic rise in fortunes.

Chart 1 at the back of this book shows the family relationship between Victoria and Albert, who were first cousins; her mother and his father were brother and sister. They came from the little German state of Saxe-Coburg, which today is part of Bavaria. Saxe-Coburg was a real royal-backwater, less than twenty square miles in size and with fewer than sixty thousand inhabitants. The Saxe-Coburg family had neither money, nor great position, nor power. But astonishingly, within a period of just five years in the 1830s they acquired three thrones – Belgium, Portugal, and Great Britain; and more thrones were to follow in the future. The Saxe-Coburgs were generally good-looking and they owed their rise in the world to marrying well. Their marriage strategy was so successful that Saxe-Coburg was named *the stud farm of Europe.*

5. The formidable dowager Duchess Augusta of Saxe-Coburg, grandmother of both Victoria and Albert.

The rise of the Saxe-Coburg family was founded on the marriages of one generation – the seven brothers and sisters who included Albert's father and Victoria's mother. They were the children of Duke Franz Friedrich Anton of Saxe-Coburg-Saalfeld, who died in 1806, and his second wife Duchess Augusta (1757-1831), who was a formidable lady and the power behind the throne in the family. Chart 2 shows the thrones which descended from the marriages of her children.

Albert's father was Duke Ernst I of Saxe-Coburg (the eldest son of Duchess Augusta) and his mother was Duchess Luise, an heiress from the next-door little state. They married in 1817. It was a good match for Ernst because Luise was the only child of the reigning duke of Saxe-Gotha-Altenburg (Saxe-Gotha for short) and second in line (after her uncle, who was in his forties and unmarried) to inherit the duchy. She brought a substantial dowry to the marriage, and also fulfilled her dynastic duty by quickly producing two sons – Ernst junior in 1818 and Albert in 1819.

6. Schloss Rosenau in Coburg where Albert was born.

The role of Victoria's uncle – Leopold of Saxe-Coburg

Leopold of Saxe-Coburg (born in 1790), was the youngest of the seven surviving children of Duchess Augusta. His life changed after he visited London in 1814 with Tsar Alexander I of Russia (one of Leopold's older sisters had married Alexander's brother) and he met Princess Charlotte of Great Britain. Charlotte was the only child of the prince regent (later George IV) and the next heir to the British throne after her father. She had just jilted the fiancé selected by her father and thought she was in love with another prince who did not meet with her father's approval. As a younger son from a small German duchy, Leopold's chances did not look much better, but amazingly he and Charlotte fell in love, the prince regent gave his consent, and they were married in 1816.

Their happiness was short-lived. Charlotte died in November 1817 giving birth to their first child, a stillborn son. Leopold had been genuinely in love and was devastated by grief; he stayed on in England as a widower. But as time passed his ambition re-emerged and in 1831 Leopold became the first king of Belgium, a new country just made independent of the Netherlands. The descendants of King Leopold 1 still sit on the Belgian throne today. King Philippe is Leopold's great-great-great-grandson.

Leopold was the driving force behind another Saxe-Coburg throne when he arranged the marriage of another of his sisters, Victoire (born in 1786), to Edward Duke of Kent (the fourth son of George III), in 1818. This marriage was important because, after Charlotte's death, any children would be in the running for the British throne. The first part of **The Colourful Life of Queen Victoria** (called **Young Victoria**) tells the story of the race to produce the next heir, and how the only child of Edward and Victoire, born on 24 May 1819, was Queen Victoria.

After the death of the duke of Kent in January 1820, Leopold became a father figure and mentor to his little niece. But after she came to the throne Victoria was less inclined to listen to her uncle's advice, and his role as mentor was replaced, initially by her first prime minister, Lord Melbourne (see **Young Victoria**), and later by her husband, Albert.

7. Victoria wearing a bracelet with a miniature painting of Albert.

But the marriage was unhappy almost from the start. There was a big age-gap between the couple; Luise was sixteen years old when they married and Ernst thirty-three. Also he was a long-time womaniser who had a scandalous affair in his past which had helped to scupper a much grander royal engagement to the sister of Tsar Alexander I. In her memoirs published in 1823, one of his ex-lovers accused Ernst of seducing her when she was fifteen and then abandoning her and their child[1]. Courtiers made sure they passed on the stories of her husband's infidelities to Luise, and soon she was complaining of loneliness and writing to Ernst to remind him of his marriage vows and that 'Pleasuring yourself with another cannot truly please you, since it is sinful'[2].

Ernst saw no reason to change his ways. Aristocratic men like him were not expected to be faithful; besides he had married Luise for her money and not for love. Luise was a nice girl and she seems to have started off with the best intentions. But she was young, romantic, lonely, and badly treated by her husband. She began to enjoy flirtations with other men and there were rumours that she was unfaithful. What was sauce for the gander was definitely not sauce for the goose; Ernst could not tolerate his wife's infidelity and insisted on a separation. In 1824 Luise was sent away and the terms of the separation were harsh; she was not permitted to see her sons and was given only an allowance whilst Ernst kept control of her fortune.

So Albert came from a broken home; his mother disappeared overnight when he was five years old and he never saw her again. The trauma of this forced separation must have had an effect on him. He grew up undemonstrative and reserved, and, some of his contemporaries said, with an aversion to women. Both his father and his brother were libertines, but Albert was different. He never looked at any woman other than his wife and was completely faithful to Victoria. During their engagement, Victoria commented to her Prime Minister, Lord Melbourne, on Albert's dislike of ladies and he suggested that this sort of thing tended to come later. Victoria scolded him, and she was quite right – it never did with Albert[3]. His disapproval of sexual immorality was one

8. Albert in military uniform at the time of his marriage.

of the reasons why Albert was disliked by the English aristocracy, who considered him a prig and a prude.

What happened to Albert's mother?

After her separation from Ernst, Luise was sent to live in the town of Sankt Wendel, in the Saarland (near the French border), some two hundred and fifty miles away from Coburg. The town was part of the small principality of Lichtenberg which had been awarded to Ernst at the Congress of Vienna after the Napoleonic Wars.

As well as her fortune, Ernst wanted to get his hands on his wife's inheritance from the duchy of Saxe-Gotha, so he waited until after her uncle (the last duke of Saxe-Gotha) died in early 1825 before going for a divorce. In the reshuffle of lands that followed the death of the last duke, Ernst was awarded a large chunk of Saxe-Gotha.

Ernst and Luise were divorced in March 1826, and six months later Luise married Maximilian von Hanstein, with whom she had begun to live soon after her separation from Ernst. Her new husband was ennobled by another of Luise's uncles so that she became countess von Poelzig. The couple were popular in Sankt Wendel where they took part in the social life and Luise gave a sizeable chunk of her allowance to charity.

Luise's second marriage seems to have been a happy one; but the couple did not have many years together. In March 1831 Luise suffered a haemorrhage at the opera in Paris, and was found to be suffering from cancer of the uterus. She died in Paris on 30 August 1831.

Prince Albert, the second son of Ernst and Luise, was born on 26 August 1819, three months after his cousin Victoria (born on 24 May). The babies were delivered by the same midwife. Fräulein Siebold travelled from Germany to England with the duchess of Kent for her confinement at Kensington Palace; and following the duchess' safe delivery, returned to Coburg for the confinement of her sister-in-law, Luise. The Saxe-Coburg family were very alive to the opportunity presented by baby Victoria's place in the English succession and plotted her marriage with Albert from a young age. His older brother Ernst would inherit the duchy of Saxe-Coburg and Albert would marry Victoria and become king consort of Great Britain. Albert himself was told when he was still a toddler that someday 'the little English Mayflower' (Victoria was born in May) would be his wife[4].

So the marriage was heavily promoted by the dowager Duchess Augusta (the grandmother of both Victoria and Albert), her daughter the duchess of Kent, and her son King Leopold I of Belgium. This was much to the fury of the British royal family, who disliked the Coburgs and regarded them as pushy upstarts. They had their own candidates and thought that Victoria should marry a prince from another major power, rather than a minor German duke. There was much manoeuvring and bickering throughout

9. Commemorative picture for the wedding of Victoria and Albert.

Victoria's teenage years, with each side trying to push their candidate forward and scupper the other.

Albert himself seems always to have accepted it as his destiny. Marrying Victoria would be his career and he worked hard to equip himself to carry out such a role. The worst time for him was when, after she came to the throne and was enjoying her new-found independence, Victoria declared that she would not marry for years and denied she had made any commitment to Albert. But Albert had the Saxe-Coburg family good looks and, as shown in *Young Victoria*, all the queen's doubts were swept away when Albert came to Britain and the cousins met in October 1839. Victoria fell passionately in love on sight and they were engaged within days. The family's ambition was achieved and Victoria's husband would be a Saxe-Coburg.

Was Albert illegitimate?

Because of the suggestion that Duchess Luise had affairs during her marriage, the question arises as to whether Albert was illegitimate and Duke Ernst I of Saxe-Coburg was not his father. A fascinating book called 'The Coburg Conspiracy' suggests this is plausible for several reasons. It dates the breakdown of the marriage of Ernst and Luise, and Ernst's loss of affection for his wife, to the time of her second pregnancy (with Albert); and argues that she would not have so meekly accepted the harsh terms of her separation had she not thought herself guilty of a terrible offence. It is also quite true that, as a man, Albert was very different in character to his father and brother, both of whom were womanisers and sponged money off Victoria.

However, Albert was always treated as the second son of Duke Ernst and the rumours about his birth do not seem to have begun until later. This does not put the matter beyond doubt and there are other cases where, to avoid scandal, a royal husband accepted paternity of his wife's children from an affair. The youngest daughter of Duchess Wilhemine of Hesse-Darmstadt, born in 1824, married the heir to the Russian throne. Officially her father was her mother's husband, the duke of Hesse-Darmstadt; in all likelihood her natural father was her mother's lover, Baron de Senarclens-Grancy.

But while Albert grew up to be very different from his father, he did show many Saxe-Coburg traits, such as intelligence, astuteness, and purpose in life. These were also apparent in his grandmother (the redoubtable Duchess Augusta) and in his uncle (King Leopold). And of course, Albert had those Coburg good looks, which swept Victoria off her feet. To my mind, Albert was a true Coburg.

3

MASTER IN THE HOUSE

For Victoria, deeply in love, their engagement was a happy time, but Albert's feelings were much more complicated. He liked his cousin but he was not in love with her. He had come to England frustrated to be on inspection and that she had backed off their understanding; he thought in his turn about walking away. He was then bewildered by the speed at which she changed her mind and probably a bit shocked by the strength of her passion. And he was also grateful and relieved that his lifelong ambition was to be achieved. But he was to suffer a number of setbacks to his plans.

The queen's choice of husband was not at all popular with her subjects. He was German, penniless, and most probably a fortune hunter. A popular verse complained that 'He comes to take 'for better or for worse', England's fat Queen and England's fatter purse'[5]. The feeling in the country was that Victoria could have done a good deal better for herself. The British aristocracy jeered at Albert's rank as a minor German duke, calling him just a *paper highness* (instead of a *royal highness*); and the street ballads had a field day, making jokes with innuendos about *German sausages* and labelling him *A petty prince of low degree*.

Prince Albert was a petty prince,
A petty prince of low degree
He left the starved country of his birth
For a good birth in this fine countrie[6]

Street ballads

Albert's foreign birth and lack of fortune were lampooned in the street ballads that were a popular media in early Victorian times, providing news and entertainment for the poorer parts of society. A street ballad, sung to a well-known tune, could be written, printed, and performed on the London streets, in not much more than an hour.

Here is a verse from a ballad called 'The Royal Marriage'; published during Victoria's engagement and sung to an older tune called 'Vicar and Moses'. The scenario is that the queen has called a Privy Council to announce her marriage, telling them... 'And my cousins before, Have had Germans by score, I'll enjoy the same recreation'. She continues

So John Bull may laugh,
And the Radicals chaff,
For Prince Albert to me is a treat;
Him I'll have in a crack,
With no shirt on his back,
Or stockings and shoes to his feet.

When the Privy Council ask Albert about his financial affairs he responds that '...And I can bring to you, And that annually too, A shipload of fine German sausages'[7].

Albert's unpopularity, and Victoria's concern not to make this worse, led to a number of frustrations for him during the engagement. First there was the question of his rank. Albert was only a second-rate royal – a mere *serene highness* rather than the higher ranking *royal highness*. There was a huge distinction between the two at the time. He

10. These portraits of Victoria and Albert, from soon after their marriage, are very early colour prints.

did receive the much coveted *royal highness* status on his marriage, but he did not get a British dukedom or any other British title. He might have expected to become *king consort* in the same way that a German princess marrying a king of England would have become queen. Victoria desperately wanted this for him – 'Oh! If only I could make him King' she wrote in her journal[8]. But it would have required an Act of Parliament and she was advised that, as the marriage was so unpopular, this could not be pushed through. Albert had to wait seventeen years for the title (until June 1857) and then it was only *prince consort* rather than *king consort*.

In the meantime Albert was just a German duke and this lack of rank meant he was down the order of precedence, which caused continual irritations and pinpricks. Victoria wanted him to take precedence directly after her, so he could be beside her on all occasions, but other members of the royal family refused to concede this. At the wedding of Victoria's cousin in 1843 the elderly King Ernst August of Hannover

11. The young married queen, with fashionable ringlets.

(Victoria's uncle) tried to elbow his way forward to be next to the queen. He was almost pushed over by Albert in his determination not to give up his place! More jostling followed over the order of signing the register and the procession into the celebration dinner.

Money was another issue and again Albert was to be disappointed. The amount voted by the British parliament to Leopold of Saxe-Coburg on his marriage to Princess Charlotte in 1816 was £50,000 per year. This was an enormous figure, perhaps equivalent to around five million pounds today[9]. Leopold had been married for less than two years, and was now king of Belgium, but was still receiving a British annuity over twenty years later.

Queen Victoria's jewellery

One of the causes of the bad feeling between Victoria and her uncle, the king of Hannover, was their long-running dispute over the royal jewels. When George III married Queen Charlotte in 1761 he gave her a wonderful wedding gift of expensive jewels and in her will Charlotte left these

> ...to the House of Hanover, to be settled upon it, and considered as an heirloom, in the direct line of succession of that house...[10']

This presented no problems until Victoria came to the British throne. Under Hanoverian law she was not able to succeed in Hannover because she was female and her uncle, the next male in the family, became king there instead. As head of the House of Hannover, King Ernst August claimed Queen Charlotte's jewels. Victoria counterclaimed on the grounds that they had been bought by George III with British money. The dispute dragged on for twenty years, even after the king's death. Eventually it was settled in favour of Hannover and the jewels handed over to his son.

Although she regretted the loss of the Hanoverian jewels, Victoria had by then built up her own collection, considerably helped by Albert's interest and good taste in jewellery. He reset some existing jewels for her and also designed and gave her some wonderful new pieces. These included the spectacular sapphire and diamond brooch that was his wedding present, and a gorgeous set made of gold and porcelain in the design of orange blossom, including brooches, earrings and a tiara. Albert gave her the first brooch while they were engaged and later added to the set. Victoria loved them and usually wore them on her wedding anniversary.

The modelling of the tiara on orange blossom reflects a fashion in Victorian times for ladies wearing wreaths made of fresh flowers in their hair. Dahlias were a great favourite for this. One of the queen's ladies with her on a royal visit to the King of France in 1845 wrote how one of the French maids asked each day about the colour of the ladies evening dresses, so that she could get the gardener to cut dahlias to make fresh wreaths for their hair.

Another Saxe-Coburg, the duchess of Kent, was also drawing a handsome sum each year from the British treasury. Parliament baulked at yet another drain on the country's resources in favour of a penniless Saxe-Coburg. For Albert the Tory opposition put down an amendment to reduce the figure nearly by half, to £30,000, and this was carried. Victoria railed against the 'vile, confounded, infernal Tories[11]' in her journal and threatened to refuse to invite them to the wedding. Victoria and Albert were forced to accept the reduction, but it rankled.

12. Presentation of an address from the University of Oxford in the throne room at Buckingham Palace.

But perhaps the biggest disappointment for Albert lay in the appointment of his personal staff. He thought this was important because of the role he expected to play in state affairs and he wanted to bring some chosen staff with him from Coburg. Victoria, knowing that her subjects would not like any suggestion of foreign interference, vetoed this.

After the wedding, the couple went to Windsor Castle for their honeymoon. This was a blissful time for Victoria and she wrote in her journal about how Albert helped her to put on her stockings and she watched him shave.

> ...how can I ever be thankful enough to have such a <u>Husband</u>!... to lie by his side, and in his arms...and be called by names of tenderness, I have never yet heard used to me before – was bliss beyond belief!
> ...his love and gentleness is beyond everything, and to kiss that dear soft cheek, to press my lips to his, is heavenly bliss.[12]

But she restricted the honeymoon to just three days and even then invited people in for the evenings. Albert had wanted a much longer time and alone, so they could get to know each other, but she claimed it was impossible because of her position.

Back in London there were more frustrations. Albert expected to be an equal partner in their marriage and had studied diligently to be able to help the queen by sharing her duties. But Victoria positively did not want his help. She continued to see her ministers alone and refused to show him any official papers. He found it hard to deal with this idleness and lack of purpose. He was also unhappy about her private life. Victoria was estranged from her mother, the duchess of Kent, and her strongest relationship was with her old governess, Louise Lehzen, who was her closest confidant and ran her private household. Albert and Lehzen were immediately jealous of each other and the scene was set for a battle between them. Albert complained to a friend that 'I am only the husband and not the master in the house'[13].

13. Louise Lehzen, Victoria's old governess.

14. Victoria was essentially a Hanoverian; warm and loving but also stubborn, emotional, and self-centred.

There were stormy scenes between the couple and an on-going power struggle over who would be the dominant partner. Perhaps this is not surprising, given their different characters. Victoria was essentially a Hanoverian; she was warm and loving, but also stubborn, emotional, and self-centred. She would pursue Albert from room to room, trying to provoke a row. Albert on the other hand was more reserved, cool, and logical; he never did anything without carefully thinking it through. He was horrified at the thought that Victoria might turn out like her Hanoverian uncles (the scandal-ridden sons of George III). So Albert would retreat from her and wait for things to cool down, and then put his side of the case in writing.

In 1934 the playwright Laurence Housman published a biography of Victoria in the form of a play. This was initially censored, on the grounds that no British sovereign could be played on the stage until one hundred years after their accession. So Housman had to wait until 1937 (one hundred years after Victoria's accession) before the play could be performed. It includes a scene where, early in their married life, Victoria and Albert make up after a quarrel. This scene was shown very effectively in the 2009 film *Young Victoria*, with screenplay by Julian Fellowes. Albert has retreated to his study and locked himself in. Victoria beats violently on the door;

The Queen:	Open the door! Albert, open the door!
Albert:	Who is that speaking?
The Queen:	Her Majesty, the Queen!
Albert:	Her Majesty, the Queen, must wait.

An angry Victoria can hardly believe her ears, but after a while she calms down and knocks on the door again, this time timidly.

| *Albert:* | Who is there? |
| *The Queen:* | Your Wife, Albert! Your poor, unhappy little Wife! |

Albert opens the door and Victoria flings herself into his arms[14].

And it was Albert who emerged dominant in the relationship. Victoria was desperately in love and she wanted him to be happy. Also, as a legacy from her unhappy childhood, she had a deep-seated need for a strong male figure to lean on – to replace the father who had died when she was a baby. So Victoria soon came to rely on Albert more and more and they took on the roles of teacher and willing pupil. After a scene Albert would point out her faults and character flaws and she would promise to try to be better. He was helped by her constant pregnancies, when she was forced to hand over some of her duties to him. It was an important moment for him when, during her first pregnancy, he was made

15. Albert was reserved, cool, and logical, to my mind a true Coburg.

23

regent for his unborn child in case Victoria should die in childbirth; also when shortly after the birth in November 1840, she handed him the key to her official despatch boxes.

The first attempt on Victoria's life

Illustration 16 depicts the first of eight assassination attempts on the queen's life during her reign. In June 1840, a few months after their marriage, Victoria and Albert were out for their usual afternoon drive in an open carriage, when a young man called Edward Oxford fired two pistols at her on Constitution Hill near Buckingham Palace. The picture shows Albert flinging his arm around his pregnant wife after the first shot, to pull her down in the carriage. The would-be assassin was surrounded by the crowd and arrested by a police constable.

Edward Oxford was eighteen years old and unemployed. He had previously worked in a pub in a job known as 'pot-boy'. At his trial it was not clear if the pistols were loaded and he later claimed that he had not really intended to harm the queen. He was found 'not guilty on the ground of insanity' and incarcerated in Bethlem hospital for the insane and later in Broadmoor.

In 1867 Oxford was released on condition that he emigrated and never returned. He went to Australia under an assumed name where he later married and became a respectable pillar of Melbourne society. Edward Oxford died in 1900.

But Albert's complete victory came only when he was finally able to force the retirement of Victoria's ex-governess. Louise Lehzen had been everything to Victoria during her childhood and remained very close to her. But she was a jealous woman and after the marriage her nose was out of joint as Albert took first place with Victoria. Lehzen unwisely chose to try to undermine Albert, rather than adapt to him, and was a source of bitter discord between the couple. Albert wrote to a family friend who tried to mediate between the warring couple;

16. Edward Oxford fires at the pregnant queen
while she is out driving with Albert.

Victoria is too hasty and passionate for me to be able often to speak of my difficulties. She will not hear me out but flies into a rage and overwhelms me with reproaches of suspiciousness, want of trust, ambition, envy etc etc...All the disagreeableness I suffer comes from the same person [Lehzen] and that is precisely the person whom Victoria chooses for her friend and confidant [15].

In response Victoria defended her position, claiming that she seldom saw her old governess now and that Albert could not object to her having Lehzen to talk to [16].

It was inevitable that Albert would win this battle, but it took him nearly three years. Not until September 1842, when Victoria was still suffering post-natal depression after the birth of her second child, could she be brought to the point; and Lehzen was retired back to Germany with a pension.

Albert was now master in the house. He had learned how to manage his wife's more volatile character, although dealing with her outbursts would always be a strain. From now on Albert's role would grow until he was effectively joint monarch and absolutely everything to Victoria – husband and best friend, mentor and father figure, private secretary and adviser. Victoria could not do anything without him, and that would be a real issue in her inability to cope with his early death.

4

THE SHADOW SIDE

Between 1840 and 1857 Victoria and Albert had nine children, and the story of their marriage is as much about family life as it is about government and affairs of state.

Victoria did not want to have a big family. She wanted to wait before having children and was therefore furious to find herself pregnant within weeks of the wedding. Her first child, Victoria, Princess Royal, was born in November 1840. Her parents affectionately called her Pussy as a baby, but later on she would always be Vicky. Both Victoria and Albert had hoped for a boy, and were therefore disappointed. 'Never mind, the next will be a prince.'[17] said the queen, after she was told the baby's sex. But Vicky was an enchanting child – intelligent and quick to learn, if somewhat naughty. She would always be her father's favourite.

After Vicky's birth, Victoria wrote to her uncle King Leopold I of the Belgians

> I think, dearest Uncle, you cannot *really* wish me to be the 'Mama d'une *nombreuse* famille' [Mother of a big family].... men never think, at least seldom think, what a hard task it is for us women to go through this *very often*.[18]

17. Vicky as a baby with her nurse.

So she was therefore even more horrified to find herself pregnant again, only weeks after the birth of Vicky. And this second pregnancy did not go so smoothly. Victoria felt unwell, had a more difficult birth and suffered from post-natal depression afterwards, as she would with her later children. And it was made worse because this was the period of constant rows with Albert over Lehzen. Victoria' second child, born just less than a year after his sister in November 1841, was Albert, Prince of Wales, always known as Bertie. The portrait in illustration 18 shows the queen with her two eldest children, when Bertie was just a few weeks old.

So, before she had been married for two years, Victoria had two children. Many years later she wrote to her eldest daughter, Vicky, who was just married herself

What made me so miserable was – to have the two first years of my married life utterly spoilt by this occupation! I could enjoy nothing – not travel about or go about with dear Papa and if I had waited a year, as I hope you will, it would have been very different[19].

Of course her daughter didn't wait. Vicky also had two babies before she had been married for two years.

Victoria dreaded her pregnancies. Victorian ladies were told to avoid any exertion and she resented giving up things that she enjoyed, like riding, dancing, and parties. Doctors also cautioned against sex during pregnancy claiming that this could damage the health and morals of the unborn baby. Victoria would have found this very difficult too as she enjoyed the physical side of her relationship with Albert.

Giving birth in Victorian times was a risky business. In the middle of the nineteenth century (by which time record-keeping had become reliable), the statistics show death rates in England and Wales at almost five per cent, or one in twenty women. The three big killers were infection, haemorrhage, and convulsions (eclampsia), and the causes and treatment of these were not yet fully understood. In an age when we do not expect anyone we know to die in childbirth, it is hard to imagine the real terror that must have gripped some young women as they approached their confinements.

18. Victoria had two babies before she had been married for two years.

There was little pain relief available and only the last two of Victoria's nine children were born with the help of chloroform. The queen became a pioneer in the use of anaesthetics in childbirth when she was given chloroform during labour with her eighth child, Leopold, born in 1853. Critics attacked the practice, arguing that it was contrary to God's will, but the queen described it as '...soothing, quieting and delightful beyond measure'[20]. For her it was 'that blessed chloroform'.

19. Vicky, princess royal (born 1840), and Bertie, prince of Wales (1841).

After each birth, Victoria was confined to bed for two or three weeks (called *lying-in*), under the care of her monthly nurse, Mrs Lilly. A monthly nurse was a type of early mid-wife, who would arrive before the birth, help with the delivery, and stay on for the lying-in period. Mrs Lilly looked after the queen during all her confinements and Victoria had great confidence in her. But she was always pleased to see Mrs Lilly go because this represented the end of her ordeal and the resumption of her normal life.

Although her mother, the duchess of Kent, had breast fed her, Victoria did not breast-feed her own children. When the princess royal was born three weeks early, nothing was ready and a page had to be sent over to the Isle of Wight to fetch the wet-nurse. Because Victoria did not breast-feed she did not have the protection this might have provided against another pregnancy. Presumably her doctors did not understand, or did not explain to her, that breast-feeding can suppress ovulation and is nature's contraceptive. Her decision not to breast-feed may have been because her duties as monarch made this difficult, but it is more likely due to her repugnance at the physical process of childbearing, which she compared to '...our being more like a cow or a dog...'.[21] Later she tried hard to persuade her daughters against breast-feeding. When Vicky was pregnant for the first time her mother wrote

> I know you will not forget, dear, your promise not to engage in 'baby worship' or to neglect your other duties in becoming a nurse [ie breast-feeding]...No lady, still less a Princess, is fit for her husband or for her position, if she does that.[22]

What was a wet-nurse?

A wet-nurse was a woman who was hired to suckle another woman's baby. This ancient profession goes back thousands of years and was a common practice until the introduction of safe and reliable feeding bottles and formula milk in the second half of the nineteenth century. New mothers might hire a wet-nurse because they were unable to feed their baby or, if they were aristocratic, because it was considered unfashionable and interfered with the social round. When the duchess of Kent breast-fed baby Victoria in 1819, this was unusual for a royal lady. But by the time Victoria's own children were born in the 1840s and 1850s, things were changing.

Wet-nursing was one of the few well-paid jobs available to poor women. Unfortunately this could sometimes lead to tragic consequences, such as women getting rid of their own babies before seeking employment as a wet-nurse. In later centuries it became a well-organised and regulated profession, although still with some undesirable outcomes, such as the use of alcohol or opium products to keep babies quiet. A cartoon in 1842, after the birth of the prince of Wales, shows Victoria and Albert discovering his wet-nurse pouring strong drink down the baby's throat. Wet nursing had died out by 1900.

In Victoria's time, death in childbirth was a constant threat and child mortality rates were high. So she was fortunate that she survived her constant pregnancies with no lasting damage to her health and that all of her children lived to be adults. But her dislike of what she called *the shadow side* of marriage made her sympathetic to the lot of women in this respect.

> I had 9 times for 8 months to bear with ... real misery...and I own that it tried me sorely; one feels so pinned down – one's wings clipped...only half oneself...This I call the 'shadow side'...And therefore – I think our sex a most unenviable one[23].

20. This charming picture shows Victoria and Albert with their children playing around them; baby number six (Louise, 1848) is in the cradle.

Chart 3 at the back of this book has a list of Victoria's nine children with brief details about their lives. Like their mother, many of them also have colourful stories and there will be more about these in the next book – *The Widowed Queen: The Colourful Personal Life of Queen Victoria – Part 3*.

5

MY BELOVED ALBERT

Victoria was a talented artist and there are albums in the royal collection of her drawings and paintings of her children from the birth of Vicky up to Albert's death. Illustration 21 is a reproduction of her drawing of her three eldest children – Vicky, Bertie and Alice – in 1845. No one looking at her pictures can doubt that Victoria loved her children, or that she was deeply interested in the little details of their lives. But she was not naturally maternal and her happiness in family life was based on Albert's delight in being a father. For Victoria, Albert always took first place and perhaps she felt some resentment about his time and attention that their children took away from her.

Albert was delighted to be the father of a large family. Family life was important to him, perhaps because of his early loss of his mother. He was a good father, who enjoyed spending time with his children. Albert has come down in history as a worthy but rather dull character, so that it is endearing to know that he liked to get down on the nursery floor and play games. The prince arranged family outings, and took the children on trips to the theatre, circus, the zoo, and Madam Tussauds. The royal children saw much more of their parents than was common for the aristocracy at that time. Birthdays and anniversaries were celebrated with parties and presents, and the children put on tableaux and shows for their parents. On Victoria and Albert's fourteenth wedding anniversary in February 1854, the children dressed up as *The Four Seasons*, with Bertie as Winter, Vicky as Spring, and the next two in age, Alice and Alfred, as Spring and Summer.

21. Print from a drawing by Victoria of her three eldest children,
Vicky, Bertie and Alice.

Christmas was always spent at Windsor Castle and was another great family occasion. Albert wanted Christmas for his children to be like those he remembered from his own childhood in Coburg. The royal family's rooms were filled with Christmas trees decorated with sweetmeats and candles, including one in the nursery for the children. Despite what is often said, Albert did not introduce the German custom of a Christmas tree to England (it had already arrived sometime before) but he and Victoria did popularise its use. After it got dark on Christmas Eve, the candles on the tree were lit and the family exchanged presents from a table laden with gifts (Queen Elizabeth II and her family still follow the German custom of giving presents on Christmas Eve.) On

Christmas day there was a great Christmas dinner feast and over the holiday there were family games, shooting parties, and, if the weather was cold, skating on the pond below the castle.

Was Victoria a bad mother?

In modern terms, we would probably say that Victoria was a not a good mother. She actively disliked babies, referring to their 'terrible frog like action' in waving about their arms and legs[24]. Her children were handed over to others at birth to look after, which meant that there was no opportunity for natural bonding between mother and child.

In his lifetime, Albert was the focal point of the family and Victoria's involvement in family life was largely because this pleased Albert. When he died, his children lost a central figure in their lives and Victoria made no attempt to fill the gap. Her entire focus was on her own loss and she was not interested in her children's needs or feelings. Particularly for the younger children, still at home, there was not a lot of joy left. Victoria became a stern and distant figure who expected to have her wishes obeyed and to control her children's lives. Even when grown-up, they were in awe of her.

*Victoria proved to be a better grandmother than a mother. She enjoyed the company of her numerous grandchildren and also her great-grandchildren, who called her **Gan-Gan** (the name Prince George of Cambridge now uses for his great-grandmother, Queen Elizabeth II). Victoria was a support for her grandchildren in time of need. When her daughter Alice died young leaving five children under sixteen, Victoria stepped in as surrogate mother. When a granddaughter was in trouble with her marriage, the queen famously telegraphed 'Tell my granddaughter to come home to me'[25].*

Albert was determined to change the public image of the royal family and bury the shadow of the degenerate Hanoverians in the queen's ancestry. With Victoria and Albert the monarchy became free from scandal and projected an image of happy family life that was popular with the middle and working classes and much more in keeping with the emerging Victorian age. Illustration 23 shows a picture of cosy domesticity from 1850 – the royal children are playing outdoors on the East Terrace at Windsor Castle while their parents watch them out of the window.

The birth of the princess royal in 1840, and the prince of Wales in 1841, were greeted by the British public with celebrations and relief that the succession to the throne was now secure. A street ballad for Bertie's birth was called *Britannia's Two Strings to her Bow*. But as the 1840s progressed and the babies kept coming (Alice in 1843, Alfred in 1844, Helena in 1846 and Louise in 1848), concern grew louder about the cost to the country of a large and ever-increasing royal family. The cartoon in illustration 22 looks forward and predicts that by 1855 a plump and complacent Victoria and Albert will be followed by a crocodile of fourteen royal children, one for each year of their marriage. On the left representing Britain is a ragged and emaciated John Bull. (Please note that the spelling mistakes are original, from the cartoon, and done to emphasis Albert's heavy German accent.)

22. This Victorian cartoon comments on the cost to the country of an ever-increasing royal family.

Albert to John Bull:	Ah, ah, Mistare Pull, I tell you one, two, tree, fou ten year ago, I come to dis country for your Goots! [For your own good]
John Bull in reply:	Goods indeed! you have had Money and Goods too with a vengeance!

When Victoria and Albert were first married, the main royal residences were Buckingham Palace in London and Windsor Castle, a few miles to the west. The royal homes were inconvenient and badly run, with wholesale pilfering, food gone cold before it reached the table, and overflowing cesspits. One of Albert's early tasks was to reorganise the royal household, bringing this under tighter control and rooting out waste, corruption, and mismanagement.

Security was also an issue. When Victoria was lying-in at Buckingham Palace, after the birth of Vicky, her monthly nurse Mrs Lilly found a boy, who had sneaked into the palace, hiding under the sofa! Victoria and

23. The royal children playing on the terrace at Windsor while their parents watch from the window.

Albert wanted a real home of their own, and a retreat in the countryside where they could enjoy privacy, so in 1845 they bought Osborne on the Isle of Wight. Here Albert built a new house to his own design in the style of an Italian villa.

24. Osborne House on the Isle of Wight was Albert's own creation.

Osborne House is entirely Albert's creation. He was his own architect, working with the builder, Thomas Cubitt. The family wing was built with all the latest mod cons and it is amazing to see the couple's en-suite bathroom with a shower and flush toilet plumbed directly into the drains. The house has wonderful grounds with views of the Solent and a special area for the children, with their own garden plots, miniature Swiss chalet where the girls learnt to cook, and a play fort for the boys.

Osborne House is still a special place and well worth a visit. Victoria and Albert's rooms are untouched, and you get a real feeling for how they lived. After Victoria's death the rooms were sealed up for fifty years, until after Queen Elizabeth II came to the throne, when they were opened to the public. The best time to go to Osborne is in the spring, when the primroses are out.

In the 1850s, Victoria and Albert built another house at Balmoral in Scotland, where they holidayed every autumn, dressed in tartan, and threw themselves with enthusiasm into the life of the highlands, with deer-stalking, picnics, bonfires, and highland dancing. But Osborne was always special for Victoria and it was there that she retreated after the death of Albert, in December 1861. And it was at Osborne House that Victoria herself died, nearly forty years later, in January 1901.

Albert was determined to carve out a role for himself as the husband of the reigning queen of England. He was initially a puzzle to Victoria's ministers because he wasn't content to live the leisured lifestyle of a wealthy prince, but wanted to be of service to his new country. His attempts to become a working royal were at first met with suspicion and resistance. When Albert proposed to visit all the big manufacturing towns in turn, starting with Birmingham, the Cabinet gave dire warnings of the risk of public hostility, republican demonstrations, even of assassination. In fact, the visit in November 1843 was a great success, with Albert showing the common touch when, during the tour of an electroplating factory, he joked that, with their products, everyone could live like a king.

The 1850s were the years of the Prince Albert's greatest achievements. His abilities were recognised by the government and his views were influential, particularly in the areas of education, the arts, and social conditions. He was Chancellor of Cambridge University, President of the Society of Arts, Master of Trinity House (a City Guild responsible for lighthouses, navigation, and also maritime

25. Albert had to carve out a role as husband of the reigning queen.

charities), and President of the Society for Improving the Condition of the Labouring Classes (which aimed to improve housing conditions and is now part of the Peabody Trust). In 1857 there was public recognition when he was, at last, created *prince consort*.

Albert was the driving force behind the Great Exhibition of 1851, the magnificent showcase for British products and industry in the glittering *Crystal Palace* erected in Hyde Park in London. The project was fraught with difficulties but the prince surmounted all the problems and the exhibition was an enormous success for which Albert was rightly given the credit. Thirty-four thousand people attended on the first day when the exhibition was opened by Victoria, Albert, and their children, and over the eight months of its life more than six million visitors came through the doors. Despite heavy set-up costs, the Great Exhibition made a profit and Albert left a wonderful legacy when he recommended that this be used to buy land in Kensington and build museums. The Victoria and Albert museum, Natural History museum, Science museum and Albert Hall are the result.

26. Victoria visits the Great Exhibition with Emperor Napoleon III of France.

After the opening day on 1 May 1851, Victoria proudly wrote to her Uncle Leopold, king of Belgium.

> ...I wish you could have witnessed the 1st May 1851, the *greatest* day in our history, the *most beautiful* and *touching* spectacle ever seen, and the triumph of my beloved Albert...It was the *happiest, proudest* day in my life, and I can think of nothing else.[26]

27. The fourth and fifth children; Alfred (1844) and Helena (1846).

By now Victoria was heavily dependent on her husband's advice and he was sharing the queen's workload – commenting on all state papers, and drafting replies. They worked at desks side by side and received her ministers together. He was effectively joint monarch and king in all but name. Under his tutelage Victoria came to accept that the crown should be above politics and moved away from the political partisanship of the early years of her reign when she favoured Lord Melbourne and the Whigs (see *Young Victoria*). This is Albert's second great legacy – a model of constitutional monarchy that we still recognise today.

But there was a shadow hanging over their happiness when it became apparent that Victoria's youngest son suffered from haemophilia. This is a disorder of the blood whereby a component which makes it clot is

28. Grand state portraits of the queen and the prince consort in 1859.

missing, so that any cut or small injury can be dangerous as the sufferer could bleed to death. If the injury is external, such as a cut, the wound can be tightly bound to stop the bleeding. But if it is an internal injury, such as a bruise, nothing can be done. The blood continues to flow, filling the internal cavities and joints and causing deformity, fever, and agonising pain. In Victorian times there was no treatment; anyone who had the disease suffered terribly and most of them died young. Doctors and parents, however rich and powerful, could only stand by and watch.

Victoria's fourth son, Leopold, was born on 7 April 1853. Haemophilia sufferers are sometimes first diagnosed when they begin to crawl or walk (and are subject to bumps and bruises) and Leopold's first recorded attack was in summer 1855, when he was two years old. Like other sufferers, he had bouts of the disease throughout his childhood, when following a minor accident he suffered from agonising internal bleeding that left him confined to bed for weeks and crippled. There is a photo of Victoria's nine children, taken in 1865, that shows Leopold with a bent leg and propped up by a chair because he cannot stand or walk following a bout of bleeding.

Haemophilia is an inherited disease, which comes down the female line. Sufferers from the disease are almost always boys, but they get it from their mothers who are the carriers. Victoria was a carrier and passed on the disease to Leopold. Inheriting the disease is something of a genealogical lottery, because not all the sons of a haemophiliac mother will get haemophilia, nor all of the daughters carry it into the next generation. Leopold was the only one of Victoria's four sons to suffer from the disease, and only two of her five daughters were proven carriers (there are question marks over another two). Chart 4 shows how Victoria and Albert's children were affected by the disease and how her daughters and granddaughters took it into other European royal families. One granddaughter became tsarina of Russia where the haemophilia of her only son was a factor in the fall of the Romanov dynasty and the Russian revolution.

How did Queen Victoria get the haemophilia gene?

There has always been a debate about how Victoria got the gene for haemophilia. Did she inherit this from her mother or was it a gene defect that originated in Victoria herself?

The lack of evidence of haemophilia on her mother's side has influenced historians to the view that a gene mutation in Victoria was the likely cause of the disease. The queen herself was always adamant that the disease was not in her family. However, a re-evaluation of Victoria's family tree in a biography of Prince Leopold, tracing back the generations through the female line to her great-great-grandmother, has revealed a suggestive pattern of the early deaths of sons for no obvious reason. Haemophilia was not a recognised disease until the nineteenth century, so that the death of these boys before that could not be attributed to it at the time and it is at least possible that haemophilia was the cause. The debate about how Victoria got the gene is never likely to be settled with certainty.

29. Victoria with her seventh and favourite child, Arthur,
who was free of the bleeding disease.

Haemophilia was a known disease in Victoria and Albert's time, but the mechanics were not yet fully understood. Victoria's letters to other members of the family suggest she thought it could be a weakness of the blood vessels (rather than a defect in the blood itself) and hoped that Leopold might grow out of the disease. She never seems to have understood the strong likelihood that some of her daughters would pass it on.

In 1858 the family circle started to break up when seventeen-year-old Vicky, the princess royal, married Prince Friedrich of Prussia (always known as Fritz), who was the next heir after his father to the Prussian throne. The marriage was the result of years of planning by her parents. Teenage marriages were quite common for princesses in the nineteenth century and Vicky had become engaged to Fritz at Balmoral when she was only fourteen. Albert wanted a grand destiny for his first-born and favourite child. Like many German liberals of the time, his dream was to see the different German states unified into a single country under Prussia leadership. With Fritz on the Prussian throne as a constitutional monarch, Vicky was to be Albert's instrument to achieve this dream.

Illustration 30 is a portrait of Vicky during her engagement. I find this picture poignant because of what would lie ahead. Vicky was lucky in that her arranged teenage marriage would be a happy one, but all of her father's ambitions for her would be dashed. Vicky would always be an outsider with little influence in Prussia, and she and Fritz were only a side-line to German history. Germany was united under Prussia, as Albert had hoped, but it was not be the liberal Prussia of his dreams.

30. Vicky during her engagement.

It was the militaristic Prussia of Bismarck and of Vicky's bombastic son, Wilhelm II or *Kaiser Bill*, who led it into World War 1. I have sometimes wondered whether, had Albert known what lay ahead, he might have supported another German state for the leadership of Germany, such as Hannover, Saxony, or Bavaria.

When Vicky left for Prussia in February 1858, a light went out of Albert's life. I think it was Vicky, and not his wife Victoria, who was the love of his life. After she left he wrote to her very touchingly

> I am not of a demonstrative nature, and therefore you can hardly know how dear you have always been to me, and what a void you have left behind in my heart;[27]

After Vicky left, Albert began to lose his enthusiasm for life.

6

THE WORLD IS GONE
FOR ME

Queen Elisabeth II said that 1992 was her *annus horribilis*. This was the year that Charles and Diana separated and a huge fire swept through Windsor Castle. If Victoria had said it, the year she might have chosen as her *annus horribilis* was 1861, because that was the year that both the duchess of Kent (her mother) and Prince Albert died.

In the early years of her reign, Victoria had been estranged from her mother, but they had long been reconciled. After the departure of Lehzen they were brought back together by Albert and the duchess became very much part of the family circle. The duchess died at her home at Frogmore, aged seventy-four, on the morning of 16 March 1861. Victoria was with her when she died, sitting by the bed and holding her hand, but her mother no longer knew her.

This was the first time that Victoria had come so close to death and she was emotionally overwhelmed. Day after day there were floods of tears and an outpouring of grief. She was incapable of resuming her normal life or of carrying out state business. It sounds rather as if she had a nervous breakdown. She could only sit in her mother's room, go through her things and focus on her loss. She was touched

31. The Duchess of Kent in later life.

by the mementos of her childhood that her mother had kept and desperately guilty about the years of their estrangement. The finality of it all appalled her.

it is DREADFUL, DREADFUL to think that we shall never see that dear kind loving face again, never hear that dear voice again!........the talking of any ordinary things is quite unbearable to me...[28]

Her inability to work meant an increased burden on Albert, when he was already overworked and in poor health. At forty-two he was no longer the thrillingly handsome young man that Victoria had fallen in love with at sight. Photos show him as middle-aged and balding, with a paunch and a pasty complexion. His health had never been good (unlike Victoria), but by now he was ill and exhausted; worn out by the strain of his workload and of dealing with Victoria's emotions. He suffered from insomnia, stomach pains and sickness, and was racked by toothache and headaches.

He was also deeply depressed. On a visit to his old home in Coburg the year before, he had broken down in tears and said he knew that he would never see it again. Friends were concerned that if anything serious ever happened to him, he would simply give up and die. The circumstances of the weeks before he died were very unfortunate, and the reason why Victoria blamed her eldest son for his father's death for the rest of her life.

There had been jubilation when Albert Edward, prince of Wales and Victoria's heir, was born in November 1841. But poor Bertie was a worry to his parents from the start and could never live up to their expectations. He did not have the gifts of his elder sister Vicky, who was much more intelligent and quick to learn, and would always compare unfavourably in their parents eyes. He also grew up under the shadow of Victoria's degenerate Hanoverian uncles. His parents were desperate that he should take after his straight-laced and hardworking father, and not her Hanoverian ancestors.

32. The Prince Consort in 1861.

With this is mind, Albert devised a rigid regime and plan of education for Bertie. His days were filled with lessons and worthy pursuits from early to late and he was allowed little time for leisure or amusements. Of only average ability, it was all too much for Bertie. He constantly failed to measure up and was sometimes driven by frustration to temper and tantrums. Albert did not understand his son, whose failure he put down to lack of effort. His response was simply to increase the workload, which was of course totally counterproductive.

33. Bertie as a teenager.

Illustration 33 is a portrait of Bertie as a teenager. He was charming, affectionate and good with people, qualities that would make him popular with the public and a surprisingly good king when his turn eventually came. It is to his credit that, despite his parents' favouritism, he was always devoted to his elder sister Vicky, fighting her corner to the end as she lay dying of cancer in Germany. But these were not qualities given any value by his parents.

In 1861 Bertie would be twenty years old but was still very much subject to his parents' control and allowed little freedom. Over the summer he took a course with the Grenadier Guards in Ireland, but was segregated and not permitted to live with the regiment. However he was allowed to dine in the mess. On his last night there was a wild party and, as a joke, some officers smuggled an actress into Bertie's bed. Bertie enjoyed the joke; and the actress, Nellie Clifden, followed him back to Britain. Inevitably the story leaked out and became the talk of the London clubs. At the time most people might have regarded it as par for the course for an aristocratic young man, but when Albert found out in the middle of November he was devastated. His worst fears for his son were coming true. From that time his illness took a sharp turn for the worst.

The Trent Affair

The Trent Affair was the name of a diplomatic incident during the American Civil War that might have led to a declaration of war between Great Britain and the Federal States.

When civil war broke out between the (northern) Federal States and the breakaway (southern) Confederate States in April 1861, the British Government adopted a neutral position. However, this was threatened in November 1861, when a British mail ship carrying two confederate envoys to Europe was intercepted by the federal navy and the two men removed by force. The action was hailed as a victory by the federal states but seen in Britain as a flagrant violation of British neutrality, leading to demands for an apology and a show of force in return.

One of Albert's last acts from his sickbed at the end of November was to review and 'soften' the British government despatch to the US Federal government in response to the incident. The temperature in both countries cooled down, the confederate envoys were released from prison, and war was avoided.

Albert wandered restlessly from room to room at Windsor, shivering, sleepless and confused, with aching limbs and unable to eat. Until now, Victoria would never believe that there was anything seriously wrong with her husband. With robust health herself, she was never sympathetic to illness in others. But now she was desperately worried and followed Albert crying. The doctors were concerned about her mental state, so that almost until the end they played down the severity of her husband's illness. For the same reason they failed to call in any further medical help, although it may not have made any difference. Albert died on 14 December 1861 with Victoria and their elder children, apart from Vicky who was in Prussia, kneeling around his bed.

34. Commemorative portrait of Albert.

At the time and since, his death was blamed on typhoid and the Windsor Castle drains. However, his symptoms went back years, and the view is now that he suffered from a more longstanding complaint, possibly stomach cancer or even Crohn's disease.

Victoria had become totally dependent on Albert. She was not used to doing anything on her own or taking any decision without him. With his death she stood on the edge of an abyss. The force of her grief terrified those around her. They feared for her sanity and wondered what on earth would happen to Victoria without Albert. She herself expected soon to follow him to the grave and felt that without him her life was over.

My *life* as a *happy* one is *ended*! ...the world is gone for *me*!...But oh! to be cut off in the prime of life ... CUT OFF at forty-two ... is too *awful*, too cruel![29]

7

VICTORIA ALONE

But Victoria would live to be eighty-one; and half of her life was still ahead of her. After Albert's death she put aside the trappings of royalty and wore widow's weeds for the rest of her days. She retreated to the seclusion of her household and refused to appear in public or carry out her duties as queen. The public were initially sympathetic, but after a time their patience wore off; and the republican movement, with calls to abolish the monarchy, gained ground. It was only after the near-fatal illness of the prince of Wales in 1871 that she regained her popularity.

Although still a desirable catch, Victoria would not marry again. She would enshrine Albert's memory, keeping his rooms untouched, and sleeping with his nightshirt in her bed. But she would continue to look for a strong male figure in her life. Her relationship with a servant, John Brown, would become notorious, giving rise to rumours that they were lovers, or even married.

By the time she died, Victoria had become an institution. After sixty-three years, there were few people who could remember a time when she had not been on the throne. She was the symbol of Britain's global superpower status; Empress of India and the Great White Queen of

35. Albert's favourite portrait.

an Empire on which the sun never set, coloured pink on the map and covering nearly a quarter of the world's land area.

She was a great matriarch who ruled her family with a rod of iron and arranged marriages for and between her grandchildren. At the time of her death most European monarchs were related to her. It would all fall apart in the carnage of World War I, with the tragic consequence of her family being split, with uncle and nephew, brother and sister, and cousins on opposite sides. She would die in the arms of her grandson, Kaiser Bill, who as much as anyone was responsible for starting this catastrophe.

Victoria and Albert's marriage was arranged by the Saxe-Coburg family at the time they were born. They hardly knew each other before the wedding. But it would also turn out to be a love story. Albert's favourite portrait of Victoria was painted in secret as her twenty-fourth birthday present to him in August 1843. It shows not Victoria the queen, but Albert's wife, in an intimate pose with her hair tumbling down over her shoulder.

36. Victoria's favourite portrait.

Victoria's favourite portrait of Albert also speaks volumes. It was his birthday present to her the following year in May 1844. It shows Albert dressed as a medieval Teutonic knight – as her knight in shining armour.

Part 1 of The Colourful Personal life of Queen Victoria

SUSAN SYMONS

Young Victoria

THE COLOURFUL PERSONAL LIFE OF QUEEN VICTORIA

The overwhelming public image of Queen Victoria is of the elderly queen towards the end of her reign. She is serious and unsmiling, even gloomy; more of a symbol than a person. But Victoria has a colourful life story which is full of drama, intrigue and surprises. She came to the throne as a pretty eighteen-year-old; her public image was very different at the start of her reign than at the end.

Young Victoria is the first part of **The Colourful Personal Life of Queen Victoria**. It covers the somewhat bizarre circumstances of her birth, when there was an undignified race to produce the next heir to the British throne; her lonely childhood under a tough regime and without any friends of her own age; and the national adulation when she succeeded as a teenager. It ends with how she fell in love with Albert.

CHARTS AND FAMILY TREES

1. THE FAMILY RELATIONSHIP BETWEEN QUEEN VICTORIA AND PRINCE ALBERT

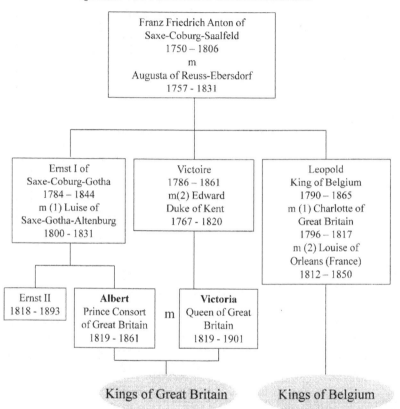

Franz Friedrich Anton of
Saxe-Coburg-Saalfeld
1750 – 1806
m
Augusta of Reuss-Ebersdorf
1757 - 1831

Ernst I of
Saxe-Coburg-Gotha
1784 – 1844
m (1) Luise of
Saxe-Gotha-Altenburg
1800 - 1831

Victoire
1786 – 1861
m(2) Edward
Duke of Kent
1767 - 1820

Leopold
King of Belgium
1790 – 1865
m (1) Charlotte of
Great Britain
1796 – 1817
m (2) Louise of
Orleans (France)
1812 – 1850

Ernst II
1818 - 1893

Albert
Prince Consort
of Great Britain
1819 - 1861

m

Victoria
Queen of Great
Britain
1819 - 1901

Kings of Great Britain   Kings of Belgium

Victoria and Albert were first cousins. His father and her mother were brother and sister.
Another brother, Leopold who became king of Belgium in 1831, was a father figure for
Victoria during her childhood

2. THE SAXE-COBURG THRONES

Franz Friedrich Anton of Saxe-Coburg-Saalfeld 1750-1806	— married— 1777	Augusta of Reuss-Ebersdorf 1757-1831	
Sophia 1778-1835	- married -	Emmanuel of Mensdorf-Pouilly 1777-1852	
Antoinette 1779-1824	- married -	Alexander of Würtemburg 1771-1833	
Juliane 1781-1860	- married -	Constantine of Russia Brother of Tsar Alexander I 1779-1831	
Ernst 1784-1844	- married – (1)	Luise of Saxe-Gotha-Altenburg 1800-1831	⟶ (see entry for Victoire)
Ferdinand 1785-1851	- married -	Antoinette of Kohary 1797-1862	⟶ Portugal, Bulgaria, Brazil
Victoire 1786-1861	- married – (2)	Edward Duke of Kent 1767-1820	⟶ Great Britain, Prussia/Germany, Greece, Norway, Romania, Russia, Spain, Sweden, Yugoslavia
Marianne 1788-1794		*Died as a child*	
Leopold 1790-1865	- married – (2)	Louise of Orleans (France) 1812-1850	⟶ Belgium, Italy, Luxembourg
Maximilian 1792-1793		*Died as a child*	

Chart shows the nine children of Franz Friedrich Anton and Augusta;
their marriages; and the thrones occupied by their descendants

3. VICTORIA AND ALBERT'S CHILDREN

Victoria, Princess Royal	- married -	Prince Friedrich of Prussia
(Vicky) 1840-1901	(1858)	*(Fritz)* 1831-1888

Vicky was the favourite child of Prince Albert, who plotted her marriage from a young age as a means to achieve his political ambitions for Germany. She was a spiky character who was always unpopular in Prussia and treated as an outsider. Vicky and Fritz waited thirty years for the throne and their tragedy was that when he became the German kaiser in 1888 (Friedrich III), Fritz was already dying from cancer of the larynx. He reigned for just ninety-nine days. Vicky had a bad relationship with her eldest son, who then became Kaiser Wilhelm II (Kaiser Bill of World War I fame). One of her daughters became queen of Greece.

Albert Edward, Prince of Wales	- married -	Princess Alexandra of Denmark
(Bertie) 1841-1910	(1863)	*(Alix)* 1844-1925

Bertie was nowhere near as intelligent as his elder sister and was always overshadowed by her in their parents' eyes. As an adult he was denied any useful occupation by his widowed mother and devoted his time and energies to womanising and high living. When he eventually came to the throne in 1901, as Edward VII Bertie proved a popular and surprisingly good king, with a talent for diplomacy. He loathed his nephew, Kaiser Wilhelm II, and drew Britain closer to France and away from Germany. Bertie's eldest son died as a young man; his second son was George V; and a daughter became queen of Norway.

Alice	- married -	Prince Ludwig of Hesse
1843-1878	(1862)	*(Louis)* 1837-1892

Alice was the eldest daughter at home when her father died in December 1861, and bore the brunt of comforting her bereaved and distraught mother. Her wedding to Louis in July 1862 was described as 'more a funeral than a wedding'. In later years Alice became dissatisfied with her marriage, her relationship with her mother deteriorated, and she suffered the loss of a two-year-old son from haemophilia (Alice was a carrier). Alice died from diphtheria when she was thirty-five, leaving five surviving children under sixteen. Her daughter became tsarina of Russia and took haemophilia into the Russian royal family. Two of Alice's daughters and five grandchildren were murdered in the Russian revolution.

Alfred, Duke of Edinburgh	- married -	Grand Duchess Marie Alexandrovna
(*Affie*) 1844-1900	(1874)	of Russia 1853-1920

Unlike his elder brother, Affie was trained for a career and left home at fourteen to join the Royal Navy. He later suffered from alcoholism and may have learned hard drinking in the navy. He married Marie Alexandrovna – the wealthy, and very haughty, daughter of Tsar Alexander I. She disliked her husband's country and his family, and the marriage wasn't particularly happy. They had four daughters and an only son, who committed suicide during his parents' twenty-fifth wedding anniversary celebrations. One daughter became queen of Romania and a granddaughter queen of Yugoslavia. Under a family agreement, Affie was the nominated heir to the duchy of Saxe-Coburg-Gotha and in 1893 succeeded his uncle Ernst (Albert's older brother), who was childless.

Helena	- married - Prince Christian of Schleswig-Holstein
(*Lenchen*) 1846-1923	(1866) 1831-1917

Helena's marriage in 1865 added to the bitter discord in Victoria's family caused by the wars between Prussia and Denmark over Schleswig-Holstein. Not only was Vicky married to the king of Prussia's son, and Bertie to the king of Denmark's daughter, but now Helena married Christian of Schleswig-Holstein, the brother of a third claimant to these territories! Christian was a poor prince, with no inheritance, and he agreed to live in England so that Helena could be on call to act as her mother's secretary. The couple had five children, including a son who died as a small baby – this is why there is a question mark over whether Helena was a carrier of haemophilia. Helena was a patron of many charities; as a needlewoman, I am especially grateful to her for founding the Royal School of Needlework.

Louise	- married -	John Campbell, Duke of Argyll
1848-1939	(1871)	1845-1914

Louise was the most artistically talented of Victoria and Albert's children and became a notable sculptress. She was also the only one to marry outside the tight network of European royalty; she married a British aristocrat – Lord Lorne (later duke of Argyll). The marriage was a miserable failure and the couple had no children (Lorne may have been homosexual), so that we cannot know whether Louise was a haemophilia carrier. She seems to have been a lively character and opinion on her among her siblings was polarised – to some she was a true friend, to others a trouble maker!

Arthur, Duke of Connaught	- married -	Princess Luise of Prussia
1850-1942	(1879)	1860-1917

Arthur was his mother's favourite child. She thought him a beautiful child and made a charming nude drawing of him, aged three, draped with a towel. He was named after the duke of Wellington (victor of the battle of Waterloo) who was his godfather and with whom he shared a birthday. Arthur joined the British Army at sixteen and served for forty years, retiring as a field marshal. He married a Prussian princess and their daughter became crown princess of Sweden (she died before her husband came to the throne).

Leopold	- married -	Princess Helena of Waldeck-Pyrmont
1853-1884	(1882)	1861-1922

Leopold had haemophilia and suffered from crippling bouts of the bleeding disease throughout his childhood. As a child Victoria considered him unattractive and accident prone, but she later came to appreciate his intellectual abilities and likeness to his father. From his teenage years there was a tussle between them over Leopold's wish to live an independent life, and his mother's desire to keep him near her and out of danger. Leopold eventually achieved his independence when he found a princess willing to marry him. Less than two years after their marriage he died from a cerebral haemorrhage following a fall, leaving a daughter, who was a haemophilia carrier, and a posthumous son.

Beatrice	- married -	Prince Henry of Battenberg
1857-1944	(1885)	1858-1896

Beatrice was only four years old when her father died. A precocious and pretty child, she was one of the few people who were able to lighten her mother's gloom. As an adult she became shy and retiring and seemed destined to remain single and act as Victoria's companion. When Beatrice fell in love with the handsome and dashing Henry of Battenberg, Victoria selfishly refused to countenance the match. But Beatrice stuck to her guns and her mother eventually gave way, provided the couple lived with her. Victoria became very fond of her son-in-law, but after ten years in the queen's household he longed for wider horizons and persuaded her to allow him to go to fight in the Ashanti wars in Africa. He died there from malaria. Beatrice was a haemophilia carrier and passed the disease to a son and also to her daughter who became queen of Spain and took the disease into the Spanish royal family.

4. THE HAEMOPHILIA GENE

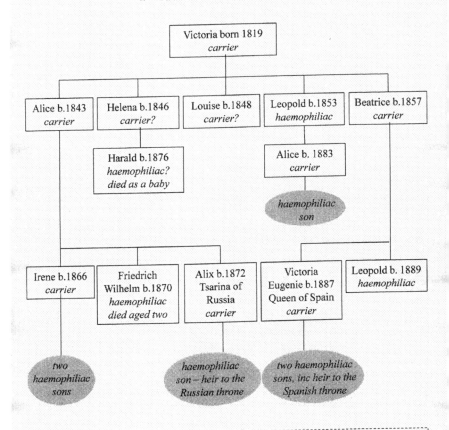

Chart shows the children and grandchildren of Victoria who are known or suspected of being afflicted by haemophilia. A question mark indicates where this is only a suspicion. Chart also shows how the disease was carried into the next generation of great-grand-children. Descendants known to have been clear of the disease are not included on the chart.

LIST OF ILLUSTRATIONS

All illustrations are from the author's collection

1. Victoria and Albert at their wedding ceremony on 10 February 1840 (after the painting by Sir George Hayter, 1842).
2. Victoria in her bridal robes, wearing the brooch Albert gave her as a wedding present (from the painting by Franz Xaver Winterhalter, 1847).
3. Albert at twenty years old.
4. *Cartes-de-visite* photo of Victoria and Albert around 1860 (after Frances Sally Day).
5. The formidable dowager Duchess Augusta of Saxe-Coburg, grandmother of both Victoria and Albert.
6. Schloss Rosenau in Coburg where Albert was born.
7. Victoria wearing a bracelet with a miniature painting of Albert (engraving by Frederick Bacon, after the picture by Sir William Charles Ross RA, 1841).
8. Albert in military uniform at the time of his marriage (from the painting by John Partridge, 1840).
9. Commemorative picture for the wedding of Victoria and Albert.
10. These portraits of Victoria and Albert, from soon after their marriage, are very early colour prints (Baxter colour prints from the 1840s).
11. The young married queen, with fashionable ringlets (lithograph by Mrs Edwin Dalton, after the painting by Sir William Charles Ross RA, 1843).
12. Presentation of an address from the University of Oxford in the throne room at Buckingham Palace (engraving after a drawing by H Melville, 1840-41).
13. Louise Lehzen, Victoria's old governess.
14. Victoria was essentially a Hanoverian; warm and loving but also stubborn, emotional, and self-centred (engraving by H Robinson, after the painting by Robert Thorburn, 1844).
15. Albert was reserved, cool, and logical, to my mind a true Coburg (lithograph by Charles Baugniet, 1851).
16. Edward Oxford fires at the pregnant queen while she is out driving with Albert.
17. Vicky as a baby with her nurse (print of an etching by Queen Victoria, 1841).
18. Victoria had two babies before she had been married for two years (from the painting by Sir Edwin Landseer RA, [1842]).

19. Vicky, princess royal (born 1840), and Bertie, prince of Wales (1841), (engraving by John Henry Robinson, after Sir William Charles Ross RA, 1842).
20. This charming picture shows Victoria and Albert with their children playing around them; baby number six (Louise, 1848) is in the cradle (The royal family at Windsor).
21. Print from a drawing by Victoria of her three eldest children, Vicky, Bertie and Alice (lithograph by L Dalton, 1845).
22. This Victorian cartoon comments on the cost to the country of an ever-increasing royal family (1855, or a Scene in Perspective: Political hits number 11, lithograph cartoon by W. Spooner).
23. The royal children playing on the terrace at Windsor while their parents watch from the window (Scene at Windsor Castle 1850).
24. Osborne House on the Isle of Wight was Albert's own creation.
25. Albert had to carve out a role as husband of the reigning queen (from a drawing by G P Nicholls).
26. Victoria visits the Great Exhibition with Emperor Napoleon III of France.
27. The fourth and fifth children; Alfred (1844) and Helena (1846) (lithographs by Thomas Fairland after Franz Xaver Winterhalter, 1852 and 1849).
28. Grand state portraits of the queen and the prince consort in 1859 (Her Majesty the Queen in Her Robes of State, after the painting by Franz Xaver Winterhalter, 1859; The Prince Consort, from the painting by Franz Xaver Winterhalter, 1859).
29. Victoria with her seventh and favourite child, Arthur, who was free of the bleeding disease (from the picture by Franz Xaver Winterhaler, 1850).
30. Vicky during her engagement (lithograph by Émile Desmaisons, after Edward Matthew Ward, 1857).
31. The Duchess of Kent in later life.
32. The Prince Consort in 1861 (after Edward Henry Corbould).
33. Bertie as a teenager (Albert Edward, Prince of Wales: lithograph by J H Lynch after Franz Xaver Winterhalter, 1859).
34. Commemorative portrait of Albert.
35. Albert's favourite portrait of his wife (from the painting by Franz Xaver Winterhalter, 1843).
36. Victoria's favourite portrait of her husband (from the painting by Robert Thorburn, ARA, 1844).

NOTES

1. *Memoirs of a Young Greek: Madame Pauline Adelaide Alexandre Panan against HRH the Reigning Prince of Saxe Coburg*. (Richard Sotnick, *The Coburg Conspiracy: Victoria and Albert—Royal Plots and Manoeuvres*, 124.)
2. Letter from Duchess Luise to her husband Ernst, undated. (Sotnick, *The Coburg Conspiracy*, 122.)
3. Queen Victoria's journal. RA VIC/MAIN/QVJ(W) Sunday 19 January 1840 (Lord Esher's typescripts), retrieved 17 July 2016.
4. The story is that Albert was told by his nurse, when he was three years old, that his destiny was to marry his cousin, Victoria. (Lytton Strachey, *Queen Victoria*, 85.)
5. Satirical broadsheet from the time of Victoria and Albert's engagement. (Helmut and Alison Gernsheim, *Queen Victoria: A Biography in Word and Picture*, 15.)
6. *The Loves of Prince Albert and Fair Victoria*. (Street Ballad of January 1940, John Johnson Collection, Bodleian Library, Oxford.)
7. *The Royal Marriage*. (Street ballad of January 1840, John Johnson collection, Bodleian Library, Oxford.)
8. Queen Victoria's journal. RA VIC/MAIN/QVJ(W) Tuesday, 18 February 1845 (Princess Beatrice's copies), retrieved 18 July 2016.
9. £1 in 1816 is equivalent to £100 in 2016. (*Historical UK inflation rates and calculator*, stephenmorley.org.)
10. Last Will and Testament of Queen Charlotte. (John Watkins, *Memoirs of Her Most Excellent Majesty Sophia-Charlotte, Queen of Great Britain, From Authentic Documents*, 621.)
11. Queen Victoria's journal. RA VIC/MAIN/QVJ(W) Monday 27 January 1840 (Lord Esher's typescripts), retrieved 18 July 2016.
12. Queen Victoria's journal. RA VIC/MAIN/QVJ(W) Monday 10 February and Wednesday 12 February 1840 (Lord Esher's typescripts), retrieved 7 July 2016. (The underlining and other emphases in the journal entries are Victoria's own.)
13. Letter from Prince Albert to Prince Wilhelm von Löwenstein, May 1840. (Cecil Woodham-Smith, *Queen Victoria 1819 – 1861*, 210.)
14. Laurence Housman, *Victoria Regina; A Dramatic Biography*, 156-157.
15. Letter from Prince Albert to Baron Stockmar, 18 January 1842. (Christopher Hibbert, *Queen Victoria in her letters and journals*, 93-4.)
16. Letter from Queen Victoria to Baron Stockmar, 19 January 1842. (Hibbert, *Queen Victoria in her letters and journals*, 94.)

17. Charles Greville diary entry for 19 December 1840. (Philip Whitwell Wilson, *The Greville Diary*, 214.)
18. Letter from Queen Victoria to her uncle, King Leopold of Belgium, 5 January 1841. (Arthur Benson and Viscount Esher, *The Letters of Queen Victoria: 1837-1861*, Volume I, 255.)
19. Letter from Queen Victoria to her eldest daughter Vicky, 21 April 1858. (Roger Fulford, *Dearest Child, Private correspondence of Queen Victoria and the Crown Princess of Prussia, 1858-1861*, 94.)
20. Queen Victoria's journal. RA VIC/MAIN/QVJ(W) Friday 22 April 1853 (Princess Beatrice's copies), retrieved 7 July, 2016.
21. Letter from Queen Victoria to Vicky, 15 June 1858. (Fulford, *Dearest Child*, 115.)
22. Letter from Queen Victoria to Vicky, 17 November 1858. (Fulford, *Dearest Child*, 143-144.)
23. Letter from Queen Victoria to Vicky, 15 March 1858. (Fulford, *Dearest Child*, 78.)
24. Letter from Queen Victoria to Vicky, 2 May 1859. (Fulford, *Dearest Child*, 191.)
25. Telegram from Queen Victoria about her granddaughter, Marie Louise. (Princess Marie Louise, *My memories of Six Reigns*, 112.)
26. Letter from Queen Victoria to King Leopold of Belgium, 3 May 1851. (Benson and Esher, *The Letters of Queen Victoria*, Volume II, 383-4.)
27. Letter from Prince Albert to Vicky, 2 February 1858. (Daphne Bennett, *King without a Crown*, 304.)
28. Letter from Queen Victoria to King Leopold of Belgium, 20 March 1861. (Woodham-Smith, *Queen Victoria*, 412.)
29. Letter from Queen Victoria to King Leopold of Belgium, 20 December 1861. (Benson and Esher, *The Letters of Queen Victoria*, Volume II, 602-3.)

SELECTED BIBLIOGRAPHY

One of the reasons why Queen Victoria is so fascinating is that there is so much to read about her. There are dozens of biographies, and these are still being written today: historians are always finding new things to say about Victoria. Even better there is a host of original material. Victoria was a talented diarist and a prolific letter writer and much of this material has been published. The list below includes some of my favourite books and also other sources used for *Victoria & Albert*. They are shown in order by date of publication, starting with the earliest.

Sir Herbert Maxwell, *Sixty Years a Queen: The Story of Her Majesty's Reign*. London: Harmsworth Bros Ltd, 1897.

Mrs O F Walton, *Our Gracious Queen, 1837-1897*. London: The Religious Tract Society, 1897.

Mrs Margaret Oliphant, *The Domestic Life of the Queen*. London, Cassell and Company, 1901.

Arthur Benson and Viscount Esher (edited), *The Letters of Queen Victoria: 1837-1861*. London: John Murray, 1908.

Lytton Strachey, *Queen Victoria*. London: Chatto and Windus, 1921.

Philip Whitwell Wilson (edited), *The Greville Diary*. New York: Doubleday, Page and Company, 1927.

Laurence Housman, *Victoria Regina: A Dramatic Biography*. London: Jonathon Cape, 1934.

Helmut and Alison Gernsheim, *Queen Victoria: A Biography in Word and Picture*. London: Longmans, 1959.

Elizabeth Longford, Victoria *RI*. London: Pan Books, 1964.

Roger Fulford (edited), *Dearest Child, Private correspondence of Queen Victoria and the Crown Princess of Prussia, 1858-1861*.London: Evans Brothers, 1964.

Cecil Woodham-Smith, *Queen Victoria 1819 – 1861*. London: Hamish Hamilton, 1972.

Daphne Bennett, *King without a Crown*. Philadelphia and New York: J.B. Lippincott Company, 1977.

Marina Warner, *Queen Victoria's Sketchbook*. London: Book Club Associates with Macmillan, 1980.

Hermione Hobhouse, *Prince Albert: His Life and Work*. London: Hamish Hamilton, 1983.

Christopher Hibbert, *Queen Victoria in her letters and journals: a selection by Christopher Hibbert*. New York: Viking, 1985.

Susan Symons, *The Image of Royalty, Queen Victoria 1837 – 1842*. University of London (Birkbeck College): MA dissertation – unpublished, 1986.

Leslie Field, *The Queen's Jewels: The Personal Collection of Queen Elizabeth*. New York: Abradale Press, 1987.

HRH The Duchess of York and Benita Stoney, *Travels with Queen Victoria*. London: Weidenfeld and Nicholson, 1993.

D.M. Potts and W. T. W. Potts, *Queen Victoria's Gene: Haemophilia and The Royal Family*. Stroud: Sutton Publishing, 1999.

Charlotte Zeepvat, *Prince Leopold: The Untold Story of Queen Victoria's Youngest Son*. Stroud: Sutton Publishing, 1999.

Leah Kharibian, *Passionate Patrons: Victoria & Albert and the Arts*. Royal Collection Publications, 2010.

Richard Sotnick, *The Coburg Conspiracy: Victoria and Albert – Royal Plots and Manoevres*. Ephesus Publishing, 2010.

Barrie Charles, *Kill the Queen! The Eight Assasination Attempts on Queen Victoria*. Stroud: Amberley Publishing, 2012.

Queen Victoria's Journals: www.queenvictoriasjournals.org. Windsor: The Royal Archives, 2012.

FASCINATING ROYAL HISTORY
Also published by Roseland Books

Schloss is the German word for castle or palace, and you are never far from one of these in Germany. For most of its history Germany was not a single country but a decentralised federation of independent states, each with its own royal family. These royals were passionate builders and left behind a rich legacy in the thousands of schlösser (the plural of schloss) that cover the German countryside.

Schloss and Schloss II by author Susan Symons each visit 25 beautiful castles and palaces in Germany and tell the colourful stories of the royal families that built and lived in them. Royalty have always been the celebrities of their day, and these stories from history can rival anything in modern-day television soap operas.

The historical royal stories in the books include the princess from a tiny German state who used her body and her brains to become the ruler of the vast Russian empire; the crown princess who ran away from her husband and six children with their tutor and created a sensation in the international press; and the insignificant princess who was passed on by her fiancé to his brother but who ended up heiress to the throne of England.

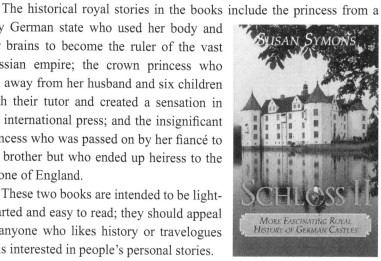

These two books are intended to be light-hearted and easy to read; they should appeal to anyone who likes history or travelogues or is interested in people's personal stories.

60191535R00043

Made in the USA
Charleston, SC
22 August 2016